Zaeden's Rainbow

This book belongs to :

_____

_____

This book is dedicated to...

 my son, Zaeden James Gregory Hoflen, who is as beautiful and bright spiritually as the many colors of the Rainbow that he found such delight in. Zaeden's brothers and sisters helped write this color-filled book especially for him.

 God gifted us with Zaeden for 2 ½ short years before he passed into Heaven. Our family experiences his spiritual closeness at heart and will always be thankful for the blessing of having Zaeden in our lives. Zaeden's fascination with learning the names of colors and constantly pointing them out to each of us is one of our family's favorite memories.

 Zaeden taught us to focus on the brilliance of life and the beautiful rainbow colors of the world around us. We hope that Zaeden's Rainbow book blesses you with joy and peace in knowing that there is nothing more important in this life than sharing precious time with those you love.

Lori Hoflen

This is Zaeden's family.

Dad

Mom

Taralyn

Schuyler

Chandler

Nolan

Kael

Adriel

Grace

Blaes

Macrae

Zaeden

We like to play Zaeden's favorite game at our farm.

Build a Rainbow

Zaeden's Rainbow

Copyright © 2012 by Lori Hoflen

Published by JHL Inc., 4314 Main St., Elk Horn, Iowa 51531

All rights reserved. No part of this publication may be reproduced, stored in a retrieval system, or transmitted in any form by any means, electronic, mechanical, photocopy, recording, or otherwise, without the prior permission of the publisher, except as provided for by USA copyright law.

Written by Lori Hoflen. Illustrated by Adriel Hoflen

Author photo of Lori Hoflen by Sue Fischer Photography

First printing 2012. Printed in the United States of America

ISBN 978-0-9845007-2-7

We each choose a color.

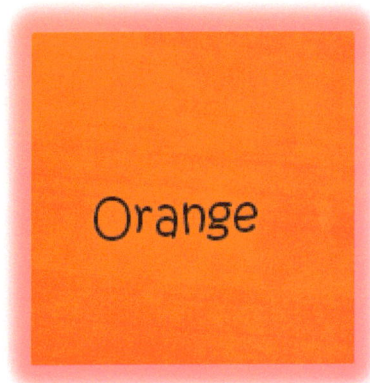

Blue

Green

Yellow

Black

Orange

Gold

Pink

Purple

Brown

Red

White

Silver

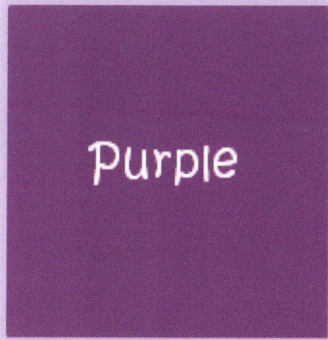

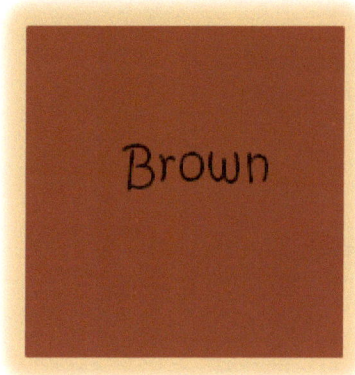

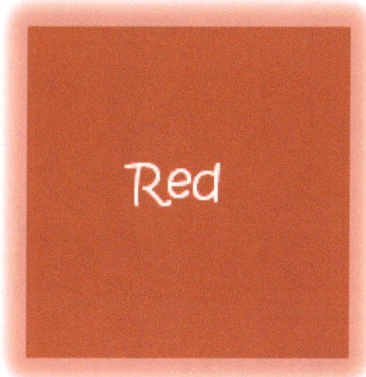

Zaeden always chooses Silver.

We run fast to
find our color
somewhere on
the farm.

Zaeden runs to play on his Silver Swing.

Zaeden is ready to
build the Rainbow.

Where is
Pink?

Here is Pink !

Nolan is feeding the Pink Pig.

Where is Purple?

Here is Purple !

Mom is watering a Purple Flower.

Where is Blue?

Here is Blue !

Adriel is feeding the Blue Birds.

Where is
Green ?

Here is
Green !

Taralyn is finding a Green Clover.

Where is Yellow ?

Here is Yellow !

Grace is chasing a
Yellow Butterfly.

Where is Gold?

Here is Gold !

Schuyler is playing
with the Gold Dog.

Where is
Brown ?

Here is Brown !

Macrae is making
Brown Chocolate s'mores.

Where is Orange?

Here is Orange !

Kael is watching the Orange Fish.

Where is
Red ?

Here is Red !

Blaes is working
by the Red Barn.

Where is Black ?

Here is Black!

Dad is feeding the Black Cow.

Where is White?

Here is White !

Chandler is finding the White Eggs.

Here is Silver !

We build
Silver and White
Clouds for our
Rainbow
to float on.

Hey, everybody!

Look up in the sky!

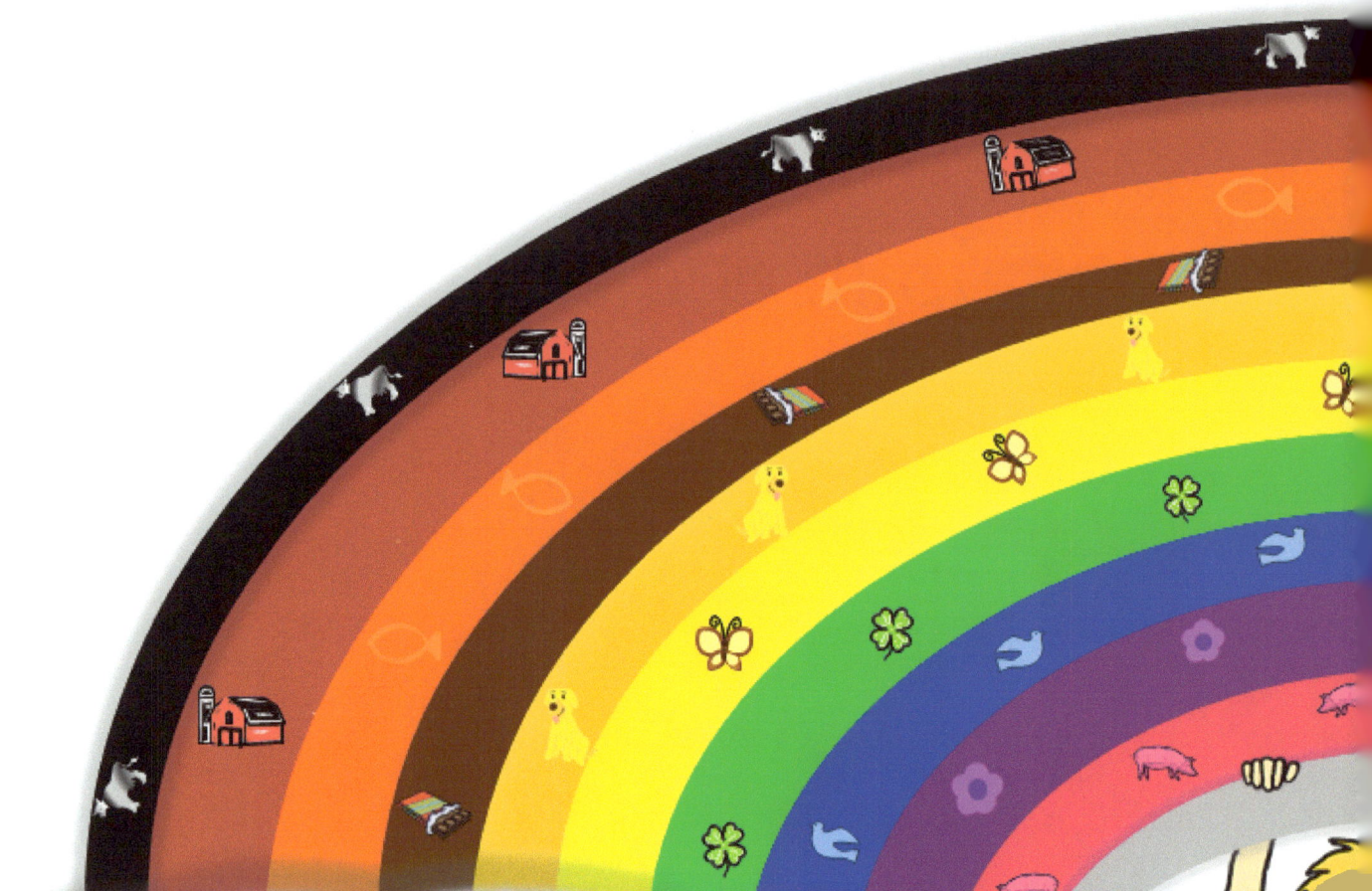

**Red
Barn**

**Brown
Chocolate
S'mores**

**Yellow
Butterfly**

**Blue
Bird**

**Pink
Pig**

Look at Zaeden's

Silver
Swing

White
Eggs

Purple
Flower

Green
Clover

Gold
Dog

Orange
Fish

Black
Cow

beautiful Rainbow !

Other books published by this Author include...

Heaven is Near... When A Child Dies

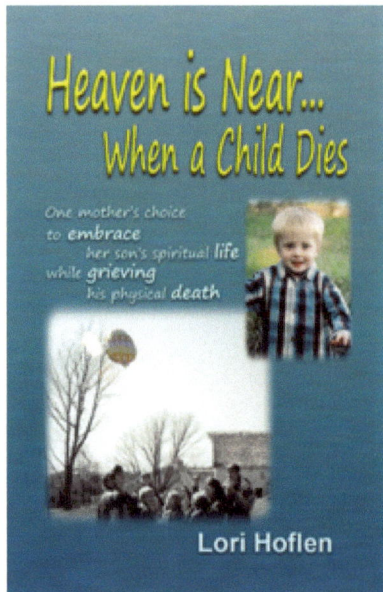

What does a mother do when her child dies and her grief is so painful that she wants to die as well?

Lori Hoflen lay in that valley of the shadow of death, yet she needs to help her nine other children cope with the death of their beloved baby brother.

The creative ways she brings her family together to honor their brother, and celebrate his life, could only have come from God. Her love and insight will be the example many families will use when they, too, experience the death of a loved one.

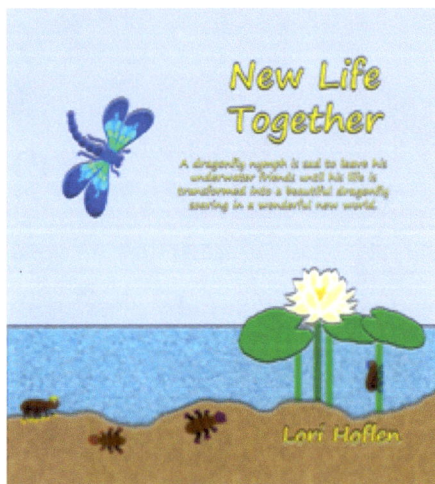

New Life Together

The life cycle story of a dragonfly nymph, who must leave his underwater friends even though he knows they are sad. They think that they will never see each other again.

After the dragonfly nymph reaches the surface of the pond, his metamorphosis into a beautiful dragonfly allows him to swoop and soar through the air, seeing the world in a new way.

His life is not over – it is more wonderful than before. He sees his sad friends through the surface of the pond and wishes they weren't grieving for him. The dragonfly is thankful that someday they will join him and soar together in their beautiful new life together.

About the Author

Lori Hoflen and husband Jim live in rural Iowa and have 11 children.

They are active Christians and members of a local church.

Lori is a volunteer EMT, coaches volleyball, teaches Sunday School, and has a Master's Degree in Software Engineering. Jim is retired Air Force and works for the Department of Homeland Security.

Zaeden has a 50' x 70' fun, colorful memory garden that the family planted and lovingly cares for at the Hoflen's farm, just four miles from their house in Elk Horn, Iowa. Each of the kids has at least one area in his garden where they've placed special garden décor for Zaeden. The garden's main pathway is in the shape of a "Z", and winds through a variety of perennials and vibrant annual flowers, under shade trees and into bright sunlit areas. There are plenty of seating and relaxation areas, with whimsical wind chimes, solar lights, and bird feeders scattered throughout. Kids of all ages enjoy the water fountain and playing in the huge sandbox with toy buckets, shovels, and dump trucks.

Jim and Lori are the founders of JHL Inc., the publishing company for this book and also founders of Hoflen Ministries, a 501(c)3 non-profit organization.

Their dream is to move their house to the farm and build a retreat center, with lodging - offering solace, comfort, and inspiration to those in need.

About Hoflen Ministries

www.hoflenministries.org

What We Do
- Speak at support group meetings and church events
- Publish, both eBooks and in print
- Gift Comfort Quilts to those grieving a loved one's death or experiencing a challenging time
- Provide Gardens for meditation and retreats
- Offer our Paintings, Sketches, and Bookmarks for purchase to support our ministry

How You Can Help
- Prayer
- Host and attend speaking engagements
- Donate — money, equipment, supplies
Donations are tax deductible.
Hoflen Ministries is a 501(c)3 non-profit organization.

Who We Are
Lori Hoflen — founder, speaker and author
Jim Hoflen — technical support, administrator and publisher
Email: lori@hoflenministries.org jim@hoflenministries.org
Mailing Address: 4314 Main Street, Elk Horn, IA 51531

www.ingramcontent.com/pod-product-compliance
Lightning Source LLC
Chambersburg PA
CBHW041236040426
42445CB00004B/51